SPOTLIGHT ON
THE
REFORMATION

Christopher Gibb

SPOTLIGHT ON HISTORY

Spotlight on the Age of Exploration and Discovery
Spotlight on the Age of Revolution
Spotlight on the Agricultural Revolution
Spotlight on the Cold War
Spotlight on the Collapse of Empires
Spotlight on Elizabethan England
Spotlight on the English Civil War
Spotlight on the First World War
Spotlight on the Industrial Revolution
Spotlight on Industry in the Twentieth Century
Spotlight on Medieval Europe
Spotlight on Post-War Europe
Spotlight on the Reformation
Spotlight on Renaissance Europe
Spotlight on the Rise of Modern China
Spotlight on the Russian Revolution
Spotlight on the Second World War
Spotlight on the Victorians

Cover illustration: An old tapestry showing Martin Luther preaching

First published in 1986 by Wayland (Publishers) Ltd
61 Western Road, Hove, East Sussex, BN3 1JD, England

British Library Cataloguing in Publication Data
Gibb, Christopher
Spotlight on the Reformation.—(Spotlight on history)
1. Reformation—Juvenile literature
2. Counter-Reformation—Juvenile literature
I. Title   270.6   BR308

ISBN 0–85078–755–6

Typeset, printed and bound in the UK by The Bath Press, Avon

CONTENTS

1 CATHOLIC EUROPE

On 31 October 1517, Dr Martin Luther, an Augustinian monk and professor of theology at Wittenberg University, nailed a list of ninety-five Theses, or statements, to the door of the castle church in the town. At that time this was the normal way of inviting theological debate between scholars. Luther's Theses bitterly attacked the practice of selling indulgences—pieces of paper which claimed to help the purchaser reach heaven by pardoning his sins. Such attacks had been made before, and certainly Luther had no intention at that moment of splitting the medieval Church. Nevertheless, his stand on that day has rightly been seen as the moment which launched the Reformation—a

When Luther displayed his 95 Theses in Wittenberg, he could not have imagined their future impact upon the Church.

movement which was to redefine the relationship between God and man, but which was also to unleash over a century of bloody religious conflict in Europe and divide the Christian Church.

Confession was a very important aspect of the medieval Church.

Religion

In our modern, secular world, it may be difficult for us to comprehend the great passions that people once felt about religion and its role in society. Today, most people take the view that religion is a personal matter, to be followed by the individual in his or her own way. Nowadays the Christian Church is divided into many branches and, although they may differ on some theological matters, in general there is a growing movement towards unity among them. Therefore it is hard for us to understand that during the Reformation, people would actually torture, burn and massacre one another because they held different religious beliefs—even though they all professed to worship the same Christian God. How do we explain some of the violent acts of the Reformation—the burnings at the stake, the Inquisition, and the spectacle of a Catholic pope expressing his pleasure at the slaughter of 15,000 Protestants by striking a special medal to commemorate the event?

No explanation will serve unless we try to comprehend the medieval mind. In a world where everyone believed literally in heaven and hell, religion and the Church naturally played a much greater role than they do in most communities today. To believe in what you considered to be the right doctrine meant salvation; not to do so meant entering the fires of hell for eternity. Moreover, the whole of medieval society, from the highest to the lowest in the land, was ordered by religion, and most people at the time felt that it was right that this should be so. No wonder that people felt strongly if their Church was threatened, or believed, as Protestants did, that the Catholic Church was denying them access to a true, direct relationship with God.

The medieval Church

Life for most people in medieval Europe was much harder and more primitive than it is today. The majority of the population lived in small villages and worked on the land, and cities and towns were still very small. Without modern medical and scientific knowledge, the people were at the mercy of diseases. Famine and plague swept across Europe at regular intervals, killing rich and poor alike. Indeed, the majority of children died before the age of seven.

For the poor, particularly, religion offered hope of a better life in the next world. So in every village the local church had a very important part to play. On Sundays and saint's days the villagers attended its services. These were held in Latin, the language of ancient Rome, which ordinary people could not understand. Instead, the congregation was expected to learn from the many images contained in the church—stained-glass windows depicting the life of Christ, statues of the saints, wall paintings and the crucifix over the altar.

Beautiful paintings were used to decorate medieval churches.

Canterbury, one of the great medieval cathedrals.

The medieval Church emphasised that all men were sinners and basically evil. Nevertheless, everyone could reach heaven if they followed the actions recommended by the Church. The priest played a crucial role here, for only he could administer the seven sacraments—baptism, confirmation, mass, penance, last rites, holy orders and matrimony—without which it was believed to be impossible to achieve salvation. In particular, only a priest could absolve a person of his sins. Before doing so, he might order the sinner to carry out certain acts of penance—such as going on a pilgrimage or paying a priest to say prayers for his soul. So important was the priest in smoothing the way to salvation, that he was seen to have almost magical powers. It was these powers that the Protestants would bitterly attack in later years.

At the centre of Catholic worship was the mass, which was believed to re-enact Christ's sacrifice on the cross. Thousands of people would cram into the great medieval cathedrals to take part in the ceremony, in order to be absolved of their sins. At a special moment in the service, it was believed that the bread and the wine held up by the priest were mystically transformed into the body and blood of Christ.

The most important clergy in the Church were the bishops. From the great European cathedrals like Canterbury, Rheims and Cologne they governed their territories and saw that the ordinary clergy did their duty. As well as serving the Church, they often acted as royal ministers or ambassadors. Indeed, many of the lower clergy also acted as teachers, clerks and secretaries, for in the Middle Ages they were usually the only educated men.

Another aspect of the medieval Church was the large number of monasteries and convents. Here, monks and nuns retreated from the ordinary world to dedicate themselves to a life of prayer and meditation. Many people went on pilgrimages to monasteries, some of which kept the bodies or relics of saints. Miracles of healing were often reported to occur at such shrines.

At the head of the whole Church was the Pope, who was regarded as the representative of Christ on earth. Ruling from Rome, the Popes maintained that their spiritual authority transcended political boundaries. Indeed, they claimed a supremacy over secular rulers which entitled them to settle quarrels between them and deal with anyone who broke God's laws or challenged the power of the Church.

Above all, the medieval Church provided a sense of unity to Europe, in what was otherwise an unpredictable and dangerous world. Every man was given his place by God, so the authority of popes, kings and nobles was seen to be divinely ordained. Because religion held the fabric of society together, it was widely thought that if its unity was broken, the whole social order would collapse. Hence both Catholics and Protestants believed fervently that religious uniformity—everyone believing in the same Church and doctrines—was of the utmost importance. And hence, also, the ferocity with which they dealt with any deviators in their lands.

A changing world
However, the rigid, well ordered society maintained by the Church was already under threat by 1500. A new spirit of inquiry and experimentation had developed during the preceding century. This was closely linked with the re-discovery of Greek and Roman literature, which revealed a world very different to the medieval one. Scholars of the Humanist movement, such as Erasmus (see page 22) were beginning to question some of the claims made by the Church. Linked to this was a growth in education amongst laymen, which was enormously accelerated by the invention of the printing press. Previously, books had been laboriously copied by hand, usually by monks. Now hundreds of copies could be printed in a few days. Luther's pamphlets, for example, were able to reach a very wide audience—this would have been impossible in previous centuries.

There were many monks who led simple, dedicated lives.

Monks were skilled craftsmen. Many were talented at calligraphy and produced hand-written and illustrated books.

At the same time, man was broadening his knowledge of the world around him. By the end of the fifteenth century, Portuguese and Spanish sailors had sailed east to India and west across the Atlantic to America. Here they encountered customs and beliefs which were very different from those of Christian Europe. These discoveries resulted in a growth in trade, and with it, the emergence of a new middle class of bankers and merchants in some European countries. These men often resented the positions of power that many of the clergy held in the governments of the day. They also began to question some of the abuses of the Church.

Misuse of power
By 1500, the Church was very rich and powerful all over Europe. Over the centuries, millions of people had given money and land to the Church to pay for prayers said on their behalf. Many monasteries had grown fat on the money given to them by pilgrims who wanted to visit their shrines. If pilgrims gave money to the monastery, they received pardon for their sins. For example, the monastery of Syon in Middlesex promised: 'In the feast of St Bridget, whosoever will come to the said monastery, devoutly there visiting the Holy Virgin St Bridget, and giving some alms to the sustenation of the same monastery, shall have pardon and clean remission of all sins.' Indeed, there was often great rivalry between different monasteries, who even tried to steal each other's relics. The papacy and higher clergy had also become increasingly corrupt by the sixteenth century. Popes like the Borgias behaved in a way that was little different from other Italian princes. They entered alliances and went to war to increase their territories. 'It was certainly a remarkable case,' wrote a contemporary of Pope Julius II in 1511, 'to behold the High Priest, the Vicar of Christ on earth, old and infirm, and educated in ease and pleasures, now employed in person in managing a war excited by himself against Christians.' Pope Leo X (1513–21) turned his court into one of luxury, pleasure-loving and idleness. He defended this with the words: 'God gave us the papacy; therefore let us enjoy it.'

Although a contributory factor, the abuses of the Church were not the main cause of the Reformation. There had always been corrupt clergy in medieval Europe—like the pardoner in Chaucer's Tale, written over a century earlier. He earned his living by selling pigs' bones to the poor under the pretence that they were the relics of a saint. But the Church's corruption and failure to reform did mean that it was unable to face up to the challenge of the new mood of inquiry. People were beginning to ask questions. Were the sacraments really necessary to attain salvation? Could the practice of selling indulgences be defended? They also began to question the whole idea of monasteries, and to ask why the Scriptures could not be translated so that everyone could read them.

As the Church refused to listen to any of this, it is not altogether surprising that some earnestly religious men began to believe that the only way they could develop the new relationship between God and man which they felt to be necessary, was by leaving the medieval Church and founding a new one.

Leo X was one of the most extravagant popes, at a time when corruption of the papacy was widespread.

A contemporary print of Martin Luther holding his German translation of the Bible, which enabled many people to understand the holy scriptures and reflect upon their true meaning.

2 LUTHER

'If ever a monk had got to heaven by monkery', Luther once said, 'I should have been he'. Martin Luther was born in 1483, the son of a Saxon miner. Contrary to the wishes of his father, who wanted him to become a lawyer, the young Luther decided instead to enter an Augustinian friary. Here he spent his time studying theology, and was appointed professor at Wittenberg University in 1508. From his own account, Luther appears to have been a devout and serious young man, yet those early years in the cloister were ones of mental anguish and religious despair. Like most men of his time, he was deeply

Whilst at the Augustinian friary, Luther reached conclusions that would challenge the accepted religious practices of his time.

concerned with the problem of his own personal salvation. Luther took seriously the Church's teachings that God was all powerful, and that therefore God alone could decide who was to be saved and who was to be damned. Yet he found it hard to reconcile this idea with other teachings of the Church which said that through their own actions of free will—such as going on a pilgrimage, or buying an indulgence—mankind could obtain salvation.

Tormented by the knowledge of his own sinfulness, Luther could not see how any action of his own (which he believed would inevitably stem from sinful or selfish motives) could possibly justify his getting to heaven. He tried desperately to make himself worthy of salvation by all the ways of the medieval Church—prayer and confession, fasting and scourging—but his doubts remained to torture him. His unhappiness was increased in 1510, when he made a brief visit to Rome and was profoundly shocked by the worldliness, pomp and luxury of many of the clergy in the 'holy' city. In the end Luther came to reject the idea that sinful man could ever get to heaven by his own actions. How then was salvation to be achieved?

Justification by faith

In a state of great mental agitation, Luther spent many hours poring over the teachings of the Bible. From the writings of the early Christians, he gradually came to believe that it was only through

For Luther, the purchase of indulgences was one manifestation of a currupt and misguided Church.

complete and direct faith in the mercy of God that man could be forgiven his sins. He found particular inspiration from a verse in St Paul's epistle to the Romans, 'The just shall live by his faith'. From this, Luther concluded that no individual action of man could help, only the forgiving grace of God. This doctrine of 'Justification by faith alone' was to become the core of Protestant ideas.

Luther's emphasis on individual faith led him to question the whole role of the Church as an intermediary between God and man. If man could gain salvation simply by turning directly to God and receiving His grace, then the whole system of the Church, designed to bring people to God, became unnecessary. What need was there to have a priest intervening in the personal relationship between God and the true believer? Instead, Luther argued that the Christian should look to the Bible alone for guidance. In this way every man could be his own priest and interpret the word of God himself. Like 'Justification by faith alone', the idea of a 'Priesthood of all believers' was to become a catchphrase of the Reformation.

Luther's stand
During the first years while Luther was formulating his ideas, he remained an obscure university lecturer. The crisis that was to change

17

his life, and tear the medieval Church apart, arose from the practice of selling indulgences. In the past, indulgences (pieces of paper on which pardons were written) had been granted to repentant sinners, who in return gave money to charity. But, as with so much in the medieval Church, this practice had become abused by the fifteenth century. Indulgences could now be bought for dead relatives. This, so the clergy maintained, would shorten a soul's agony in purgatory. A satirical rhyme of the time ridiculed this claim:

> As soon as money in the coffer rings,
> The soul from purgatory's fire springs.

Moreover, popes and bishops discovered that selling indulgences was an excellent way of raising hard cash for themselves—and the effectiveness of an indulgence soon came to depend on the price you paid for it. Man, it appeared, could now buy his way to heaven.

John Tetzel selling indulgences in 1517 to raise funds to rebuild the Church of St. Peter in Rome.

Outraged by Tetzel's mission to sell indulgences, Luther displayed his 95 Theses condemning this practice.

In 1517, Pope Leo X issued an indulgence the proceeds of which were to be used to rebuild the Church of St Peter in Rome. It was the activity of the papal indulgence collector, an unscrupulous Dominican friar called John Tetzel, that incensed Luther. He regarded Tetzel's mission as nothing but a money-grabbing swindle, and it was to broadcast his outrage that he nailed to the church door in Wittenberg his ninety-five Theses condemning the sale of indulgences. At the time, it does not seem as though Luther had intended to bring about a split in the Church, but he had taken the first step along that path, and the logic of his views was to take him to the end.

Luther denounced pilgrimages and the worship of saints, which were common practices in medieval times.

Rather surprisingly, Luther's ideas caught on very quickly. This was partly the Church's own fault because it tried to silence its angry critic. In 1518, Luther was summoned to Rome by the Pope to answer for his actions. German bishops were already accusing him of being a heretic, who had denied the true doctrine of the Church as interpreted by the popes. The punishment for heresy was burning at the stake. But Luther was also receiving much support. The crucial factor here was the printing press, which meant that his stand against indulgences reached a very wide audience in Germany. Educated people, especially wealthy bankers and merchants, disliked the power of the Church and did not approve of German money disappearing abroad to build a Roman church. Luther was given protection by his local ruler, Frederick the Wise of Saxony. In 1520, Luther published three revolutionary pamphlets which set out in full his ideas, and in 1521 he defended these ideas in front of the assembled rulers and princes of Germany at the Diet of Worms (see page 24).

In his pamphlets, Luther denied the authority of the Pope, and ridiculed his claim that he alone knew the meaning of the Bible. 'If that is so', Luther declared, 'let us burn the Scriptures and content ourselves with the unlearned gentlemen at Rome'. He denounced veneration of the saints, masses for the dead, and the practice of pilgrimages, because these stood between the individual and God. He also said that monasteries were unnecessary, and so dismissed half the Church at a stroke. For in Luther's eyes, the only job of the clergy was to help the individual interpret the word of God, and to do this they had to remain in the world. He also denied that there was anything in the Bible which said a priest should not marry—and Luther himself was to marry a former nun, with whom he lived very happily.

Forerunners of Lutherism
Despite the rapidly widening division they were causing in the Church, Luther's ideas were not new. In particular, there had always been the contradiction of whether man's fate was predestined, so that he was powerless to do anything about it, or whether he had free will to save his own soul. The founder of Luther's own order of friars, St Augustine, had stressed the idea of predestination, and many of the early converts to Lutherism were Augustinian friars.

But there had also been men who had taken these ideas further and, like Luther, denied the authority of the Pope. The most recent was a Bohemian called John Huss. He had been condemned as a heretic and burned at the stake a hundred years earlier. A crusade had been preached to wipe out his followers.

A domestic scene showing Martin Luther with his family.

Similarly, there had always been debate within the Church and pressure for reform. But by 1500, that pressure was mounting. The Humanist scholars were at the forefront of this movement. They were men like Erasmus, who were rediscovering many of the original classical Roman and Greek writings, as well as re-examining original versions of the Scriptures. The Humanists took a more rational approach, and poured scorn on what they regarded as the Church's superstitions and abuses. What was special about the Humanists was their more secular outlook. By the sixteenth century, a more literate middle class was growing up in the cities of Europe for the first time. It was amongst this class that these new ideas found a following. In Germany, especially, many town magistrates and administrators were now laymen rather than monks and priests.

The man or the hour?
The rising criticism of the Church helps to explain why Luther's ideas were received with such enthusiasm in Germany. However, although the Humanists initially welcomed Luther's attacks, many, including Erasmus, soon rejected the Reformation. Luther was neither secular-minded, nor liberal in the same way that the Humanists were.

Ironically, it seems that there was a period of great religious revival before the Reformation. Contemporary records show that more and more people were buying the new prayer books that the printing presses

The new printing presses played a vital role in Luther's campaign for reform.

The Dutch scholar Desiderius Erasmus.

were making available. An increasing number were going on pilgrimages, attending services and paying for priests to say masses for their souls. In a climate of greater religious awareness, people were bound to be more critical if they saw abuses in the Church. They were also likely to be more receptive to new religious ideas. It should be remembered that Luther was a monk, and most of the early Protestants were clergymen, so their views were respected.

Nevertheless, Luther's personal contribution to the Reformation was incalculable. He was a great propagandist and it was the strength of his personal appeal which gave the new movement its force. For thirty years he poured out books, pamphlets, sermons and letters. Not the least of his contributions was his hymn writing. There had been no such hymns sung by the congregation in their own language in the medieval Church. 'A Mighty Fortress is Our God' became the battle hymn of the Lutherans, while the children's carol 'Away in a Manger' is sung all over the world at Christmas to this day. It was in Luther's image that the Reformation took shape.

3 THE SPREAD OF LUTHERISM

If the religious climate was favourable for the new ideas of the Reformation, so too was the political situation in Germany. At this time Germany was not a single state. It was divided into some three hundred principalities and free cities which were nominally under the control of the Holy Roman Emperor. The Emperor claimed to be the successor of the emperors of ancient Rome. However, in reality the German states he was supposed to rule were virtually independent. Each ruler largely acted as he chose and this applied to individual policy on religious matters. Indeed so weak was the Holy Roman Empire, that a later French writer was to deride it as 'neither Holy, nor Roman, nor an Empire.' Whilst there was an educated class of merchants and bankers in the cities, The Holy Roman Empire also contained some of the poorest and most oppressed peasants in Europe.

In 1519, Charles V was elected as the new Emperor. By inheritance, he was already ruler of a large part of Europe. As well as ruling Austria, he was King of Spain and the Netherlands and owned large lands in Italy. Territorially, therefore, he was the richest and most powerful man in Europe, but in practice the sheer diversity of his lands made them very difficult to control. During his thirty-six year reign as Emperor, he spent much of his time defending his territories from attacks by both the French and the Turks. This left him few opportunities to deal with the cities and princes who adopted Protestantism in Germany.

The Diet of Worms
In 1521, Charles V summoned the Imperial Diet, or parliament, of Germany to meet at Worms to deal with the new religious ideas. Luther was ordered to come to the Diet and explain himself. By now he had been excommunicated by the Pope and was liable to be burnt as a heretic, so he was granted safe conduct to the Diet by Charles V.

Throughout his life Charles V remained a good Catholic, but like many others at the start of the Reformation, he probably did not realise the full implications of what Luther was saying. Luther was, after all, a monk and he was arguing about theology as monks always had. Charles V wanted to settle the dispute in the Church peacefully, if possible, before matters became out of hand.

A fifteenth century map of German principalities and towns, many with names resembling those of today. The towns of Wormatia (Worms) and Spira (Speyer) can be seen on the Rhenus (Rhine) in Badenia.

However, the situation was already so far out of hand that Luther's journey to Worms was like a triumphal procession. He was cheered and welcomed by the citizens of the towns he passed through. At the Diet, he was ordered by the representative of the Pope to recant all his ideas. Luther refused. In front of the Emperor and the assembled

Luther before the Emperor, Charles V, at the Diet of Worms, 1521.

princes and nobles he said, 'Unless I am convinced by Scripture or by right reason (for I trust neither in popes nor in councils since they have often erred and contradicted themselves) ... I neither can nor will recant anything, since it is neither safe nor right to act against conscience'. He ended his speech on a note of defiance that has become famous—'Here I stand; I can do no other: God help me, Amen'.

In the German world, Luther's appeal succeeded, and he gained enormous admiration and support for standing up to the foreign Italian Pope. But at the Diet, the Pope had his way. Luther was denounced as a heretic, his works banned and his followers outlawed. However, Charles V did not immediately arrest him. Bound by his knightly code of honour to keep his word, he allowed the heretic a safe conduct home. On his way back to Wittenberg, Luther was ambushed and kidnapped—by his friends. He was taken and hidden in a safe castle where he continued to write and publish his ideas.

The Lutheran Church

Although Luther's ideas had by now become quite revolutionary, the way he organized his Church was not. He kept the traditional structure of bishops and clergy. He also thought that the Church should be open to everyone, for while he believed that those who were going to be saved were predestined to be so, he did not think man was capable of knowing who these people were.

Luther also retained the traditional form of worship, which was centred around the mass and the offering of the bread and the wine. Although he denied the Catholic idea that these were mystically transformed into the body and blood of Christ, he did believe Christ's presence was there.

A Lutheran Church also looked much like a Catholic one. The clergy still wore robes and still administered the sacrament—though their principal job now was to preach. Perhaps the most radical of Luther's reforms was his translation of the Bible into German, so that all could read and interpret it. As a result of this, many new ideas emerged concerning religious doctrine and practice.

It was Luther's combination of conservatism and popular reforms that helped to give the new ideas widespread support among Germans,

Luther burns the papal bull—a letter from the Pope which condemned his criticism of the Church.

who were suspicious of wholesale changes in their religion. In this way, he won over many of the rulers, who then reformed the Church in their states. Luther believed it was right that reform should happen in this way, and was quick to attack more radical reformers who tried to use his teachings to justify rebellion against the established order.

Protestants versus Catholics

After 1521, Charles V was committed to destroying Lutherism in Germany. However, the many distractions in his other lands prevented him from beginning this campaign straight away. Meanwhile, Lutherism continued to spread, especially amongst the magistrates of the large independent cities. By 1526, the Catholic and Protestant states had formed themselves into opposing leagues, though it was clear neither side wanted to start fighting. They agreed to differ—each ruler being allowed to determine the religion of his territory. But in 1529, a second meeting of the Diet at Speyer again outlawed Lutherism. Six Lutheran princes and fourteen imperial cities signed a 'Protest' against the ruling. This is the origin of the word 'Protestant'.

But again the Emperor was too distracted to follow up his policies. Indeed, it was not until shortly after Luther's death in 1546 that the long-delayed war began. The Protestants were divided and badly

Luther's deep religious conviction impressed many people.

The Protestant prince, John Frederick, acknowledges defeat by Charles V following the Battle of Mühlberg, 1547.

organized whereas the Emperor had a strong army, many of them Spanish veterans of his bloody campaigns against the Turks and French. At the Battle of Mühlberg in 1547, the Protestants were soundly defeated and many of their leaders imprisoned.

However, with victory in his grasp, Charles V over-reached himself. He tried to force his authority on Germany and aroused the opposition of many of his previous supporters. Moreover, both Protestants and Catholics in Germany were disillusioned by the uncompromising attitude of the Pope at the Council of Trent (see page 44). Many on both sides had hoped that this might heal the split of Christendom.

By 1551, an alliance of both Protestant and Catholic princes had formed to oppose 'the beastly, insufferable and everlasting servitude, as it is practised in Spain', which they said the Emperor was trying to impose on Germany. Charles was even deserted by his own brother Ferdinand, who was jealous of his power. As usual, the Turks and French took advantage of the Emperor's predicament, and attacked.

Charles had no alternative but to sign a formal peace treaty with his German subjects at Augsberg in 1555. Broken and disillusioned, he abdicated to spend his remaining days in a Spanish monastery. The Peace of Augsberg gave the princes the right to determine the religion of their own territories. Lutherism was recognized, but by now more radical religious ideas had appeared.

4 THE RADICAL REFORMATION

Luther's attack on the Church destroyed one orthodoxy in religion, but failed to replace it with another that everyone accepted. At this time it was generally believed that religious unity was very important to maintain a stable society—yet the Reformation led to extreme disunity. Very soon, other preachers were formulating their own ideas about 'the true religion' and breaking away from Luther, just as he

A cartoon showing religious disunity: A Protestant preacher (left) looks to the Bible, whilst a Catholic priest (right) reveres the Pope.

had broken away from Rome. None of these different groups could agree, each trying to impose its own way of thinking on the others—often by violence. It was a period of vicious persecution.

The Peasants' War

Even as early as 1521, at the very moment when Luther was defying the Pope at Worms, some of his more radical followers were taking the opportunity to destroy the churches of Wittenberg. They believed that the paintings, statues, and ornaments, with which a medieval church was crammed, were false images which stood between the worshipper and God. Luther's authority stopped the destruction at Wittenberg. But for the next 150 years, image breaking was widespread among Protestants and often led to mob violence, as Catholics reacted angrily to defend the relics they regarded as sacred.

By 1524, some radical preachers were touring Germany announcing that the end of the world was at hand. One priest, Thomas Muntzer, declared that 'the elect' (by this he meant people who knew they were predestined to be saved) should rise up and take over the world in preparation for the second coming of Christ, which would herald the end of the world. However strange such ideas may seem to us today, it should be remembered that these preachers did have a genuine concern for the plight of the poor and oppressed. They took seriously the biblical text 'Blessed are the meek: for they shall inherit the earth', though naturally this did not impress the princes and landlords who had inherited it already. They regarded the radicals as dangerous revolutionaries.

In 1524, the German peasants, encouraged by their preachers, rose up in rebellion. The main cause of the revolt was worsening poverty, particularly amongst peasants and craftsmen, and it quickly spread across the country. Landlords were slaughtered and their lands seized. At first the peasants regarded Luther as an ally. Some of the worst landlords in Germany were the bishops and monasteries, and had not Luther single-handedly defied the Church? But Luther had too much respect for the existing social order to have any sympathy for the rebels. He vigorously denounced them in a pamphlet called 'Against the murdering, thieving hordes of the peasants.'

By 1525, the rebellion had spread to much of Germany, but it was badly organized. The ill-armed peasants stood little chance against the professional soldiers of the princes. The revolt was brutally put down and thousands of peasants paid for their disobedience with their lives.

The Anabaptists

Anabaptism was a name given to many different fringe beliefs stirred up by the Reformation. Nearly all had one thing in common—the

In 1524 German peasants rebelled against their landlords, many of whom were Catholic bishops.

practice of adult baptism of the 'elect', and a rejection of the established social order. Many anabaptists followed a rigorous moral code, denouncing property and privilege, refusing to pay taxes and sharing goods communally amongst themselves. Some groups were also ardent pacifists.

To the authorities, concerned as they were with upholding order and maintaining their own position in society, such views were terrifying. The Anabaptists were unmercifully persecuted. They were drowned by the Protestant authorities and burnt by the Catholics. The record of the trial of one Anabaptist called Michael Sattler, in 1527, shows why they provoked such fear. When asked if he would fight the pagan Turks—commonly regarded as outside God's laws by Christian Europe—Sattler replied, 'If the Turk comes he shall not be resisted. For it is written, Thou Shalt Not Kill'. He added that his captors were no better than the Turks, for while professing to be Christians, they were in fact persecuting the True Believers—by which he meant himself. Sattler was burnt at the stake.

Bloodbath at Munster

Not all Anabaptists were pacifists, however. As we have seen, some believed that in preparation for the second coming of Christ, the 'elect' should start purging the world of all unbelieving sinners. They advocated mass revolution and slaughter in the name of God.

This apocalyptical idea exploded in the city of Munster in northern Germany in 1534. The city was taken over by a group of Anabaptists who proceeded to purge it of all who refused to join them. A strange alliance of a local Catholic bishop and a Lutheran prince soon laid siege to the city, but it was defended with fanatical vigour. Inside the beleagured town, the Anabaptist leader, Jan of Leyden, had himself crowned King Jan—the New Messiah. Property and wives were made communal (there were far more women than men in the city because of the presence of many escaped nuns) and all opponents were brutally murdered. This was taking Luther's idea of justification by faith alone to ridiculous extremes. If you believed that good works did not count at all towards your salvation, you could justify almost any act you wished to.

Predictably, Munster ended in a bloodbath. The city was finally captured and the Anabaptists hunted down to the last man and woman. King Jan was tortured to death.

Even in that brutal age, the events at Munster shocked the whole of Europe. Despite the fact that King Jan's actions were not typical of his movement, Anabaptists were from then on associated with them. Many members only found refuge from remorseless persecution by emigrating to the empty areas of North America, where such

Following much bloodshed, the Anabaptists were captured and brought before the Bishop of Munster.

communities still exist. Nevertheless, although there were no repetitions of the bloodbath of Munster, apocalyptical prophets continued to foretell the imminence of the end of the world and the Day of Judgement throughout the sixteenth and seventeenth centuries. Some groups, particularly in America, still do so.

5 CALVINISM

While Lutherism was spreading across large areas of Germany and Scandinavia, a rather different Reformation was developing in Switzerland. The whole of Switzerland consisted of a collection of cities and rural areas called cantons, which were largely self-governing and independent of one another—a situation not unlike that in Germany. It was in the canton of Geneva that one of the most influential figures of the Reformation was to try out his ideas. John Calvin gave the Reformed Church an organized structure and cohesion that was to spread to many other parts of Europe—and beyond.

Ulrich Zwingli

When Calvin arrived in Geneva in 1536, Protestantism was already well established in much of Switzerland. In the 1520s, a fiery preacher called Ulrich Zwingli had begun this process by organizing the Church in Zurich along strict Protestant lines, giving it the power to supervise the morals of the citizens. However, half of Switzerland

An old print of Geneva, showing the city's churches which were re-organized and simplified by the Calvinists.

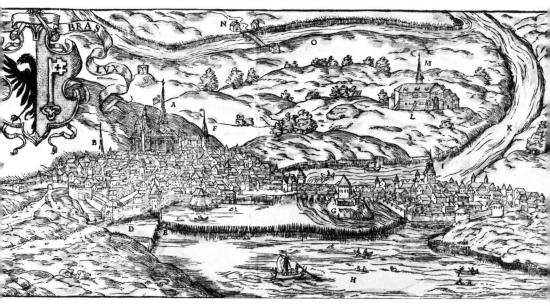

remained Catholic and hostile to the new reforms. An attempt to forge an alliance between the Swiss Protestants and the Lutherans in 1529 failed because Luther and Zwingli were unable to agree over whether or not the real presence of Christ appeared in the

The Swiss Reformer, Ulrich Zwingli.

bread and the wine of the mass. Zwingli denied any real presence, believing the ceremony was only symbolic.

Without this alliance, the Swiss Protestants were vulnerable to attack. In 1531, Zwingli was killed in battle against the Catholic cantons, and Zurich's importance in the leadership of the Reformation declined. Its place was taken by another Swiss city: 'Geneva', wrote the Scottish Protestant reformer, John Knox, 'is the most perfect school of Christ that ever was on earth since the days of the Apostles.' It was in this city that John Calvin took up the leadership of the Reformation.

John Calvin

John Calvin was in fact a Frenchman. Only eight years old when Luther was making his historic protest at Wittenberg, Calvin grew up in a world which was already divided. He studied law in Paris, where he came in contact with the new religious ideas, but was forced to leave in 1534 when the French king, Francis I, banned the reformers.

In 1536, Calvin went to Geneva, where, except for a brief two-year exile, he remained until his death in 1564. During this time he transformed the city into the stern, godly government that was to become the model for other Puritan reformers all over Europe.

Calvin laid out his Protestant ideas in perhaps the greatest book of the Reformation, his *Institutes of the Christian Religion*. For him the most important part of the Christian faith was the absolute supremacy of God. He accepted Luther's ideas on justification by faith and a priesthood of all believers, but took them one step further by stressing predestination. 'We call predestination', he wrote, 'God's eternal decree, by which He determined what He willed to become of each man. For all are not created in equal condition; rather, eternal life is ordained for some, eternal damnation for others.'

Calvin's other great achievement was to re-organize the Church. Calvinist churches were very simple. All the statues, paintings and ornaments that distinguished Catholic churches were removed. More importantly, the clergy were reorganized. Instead of being a hierarchical structure, with a head of the Church appointing bishops, who in turn appointed the clergy—as in Catholic and Lutheran churches—Calvinist ministers were chosen by their congregations. Their main duty was to preach, administer the sacraments and watch over the morals of the people. Almost as important in Geneva were the church 'elders' who were elected laymen. Clergy, elders and congregation were all seen as being equal before God.

But in this world, the ministers and elders did have real power to control and regulate the lives of the people. In Geneva they made up the supreme body of the Church called the Consistory, which could

John Calvin, whose reforms influenced the Church in many countries.

Calvinists zealously stripped Catholic churches of all ornamentation, which they believed detracted from worshipping God.

order the city council to punish sinners. Every sin became a crime. Everyone had to go to church; no one was allowed to work or enjoy themselves on Sundays, and swearing, gambling, dancing, extravagant dress and frequenting 'bawdy' taverns were all prohibited. Punishments were severe. On one day in Geneva, a court ordered a man to be executed for blasphemy, two men to be banished for drunkeness, a woman to be fined for curling her hair and a girl of thirteen to be publicly beaten for not going to church.

The French Religious Wars
Calvin very much wanted to convert his own country to Protestantism, and indeed one of the distinguishing marks of Calvinism was a strong missionary zeal. Consequently, from the second half of the 1550s, French ministers who had trained in Geneva began returning to their country to preach Calvinism. Usually picking the towns as the most

fertile breeding ground for the new ideas, they started to set up congregations similar to those in Geneva. They soon met with considerable success.

The spread of Calvinism in France was aided by the increasing political disorder which occurred following the death of the French king, Henry II, in 1559. He was succeeded by three weakling sons, and for the next thirty years central control in France fell apart. Cities, towns and even familes were divided as Protestants smashed up statues and relics, while Catholics reacted with equal violence to protect what they regarded as holy. While there can be no doubt that the religious passions of the townspeople and peasants were very real, the great noble families, contending as they were for control of the French throne, often used the religious divisions for their own political ends. For most of the second half of the sixteenth century, France was engulfed by very bloody religious wars between the Huguenots, as the French Protestants were called, and the Catholics.

The worst massacres took place on St Bartholomew's eve, 1572, when the largest Catholic noble family, the Guise, slaughtered its Huguenot rivals in Paris. Only the Huguenot leader, Henry of Navarre, managed to escape by throwing himself at the feet of the King and begging for mercy. This was followed by the massacre of Huguenot communities all over France by Catholic mobs. In a week of terror, some 15,000 Protestants were slaughtered. So delighted was Pope Gregory VII when he heard the news, that he had a special medal struck to commemorate the event.

The fighting in France only ended when the Protestant Henry of Navarre inherited the throne. Deciding that he would never be able to subdue Paris, which was radically Catholic, he converted to Catholicism himself, supposedly with the words, 'Paris is worth a mass'. But by the Edict of Nantes, Henry granted the Protestants freedom of worship and the right to keep a private army to defend themselves. However, this religious settlement did not last. The freedom of defence was revoked in 1629, and the Huguenots' religious freedom was taken away in 1685, after which Protestants were once again persecuted in France.

The Dutch Revolt
In the Netherlands, Calvinism met with more success. When Charles V abdicated in 1555, rule of the Netherlands passed to his son, Philip II of Spain—an ardent Catholic and an authoritarian ruler. When Calvinism began to spread rapidly in the Netherlands, Philip first tried to stamp it out by using the Spanish Inquisition (see page 46) to burn heretics. But this tactic provoked an angry backlash from many people, who while not themselves Protestants, feared that their liberties were being

*The spread of Calvinism in France led to the slaughter of 15,000
Protestants in one week. At the St Bartholomew Massacre in Paris,
the Huguenots were almost wiped out by the Catholics.*

threatened by the Spanish. In reply, Philip sent his able, but brutal
general, the Duke of Alba, to restore order. With an army of 10,000
troops he viciously suppressed the revolt.

However, in 1572, a group of Calvinist fugitives, who made their
living by attacking Spanish shipping, captured the northern town of

HAERLEM.

The Spanish army of King Philip II violently suppressed Calvinism in the Netherlands. This print shows atrocities in Haarlem in 1573.

Brille in Holland. Here, the 'Sea Beggars' as they became known, raised the flag of revolt against Spain. They were joined by William of Orange, a leading Dutch noble who had converted to Calvinism. The war dragged on well into the next century, and became a war of independence against Spanish rule. Eventually the Netherlands were split, with Calvinism becoming the religion of the northern provinces, and Catholicism that of the south, which remained loyal to Spain. This geographical split continues to this day, with the north forming the country of Holland and the south, Belgium.

Scotland

Perhaps the country where Calvin's ideas were put into practice most fully was Scotland—though here also destruction and warfare were employed to achieve it. There was great hatred of the Catholic Church in Scotland, for it was very corrupt and owned half the land in the country. This struggle against the Church also became associated by the fiercely independent Scots with a struggle against the French, who had taken the role of guardian of the infant Mary Queen of Scots' interests, because she was married to the French king.

In 1557, the Protestant leaders in Scotland signed a covenant to defend 'the most blessed Word of God and his congregation'. By 1560, with the help of fiery sermons by John Knox and English support, they had thrown out the French and established a Calvinist Church along the lines of Geneva throughout Scotland. The traditions of this Church still survive today in many parts of the country. Traditionally on Sundays people do not work, and until recently it would have been difficult to find a public house open.

John Knox played a key role in establishing Calvinist churches in Scotland during the sixteenth century.

6 THE COUNTER-REFORMATION

When we consider the remarkable spread of Protestantism in the fifty years after its founding, it is easy to see how the early reformers came to believe that it must be the work of God. Yet the new ideas were not adopted everywhere, and even in places where Protestantism became the official religion, there were still Catholics. Indeed, in response to the threat posed by Protestantism, the Catholic Church started a long process of reform and developed the weapons to fight the new religion to win back souls to the 'True Faith'. This is called the Counter-Reformation.

The Council of Trent

After Luther's defiance of Rome, the Catholics were faced with a dilemma. Should they try to heal the rift, or should they attack heresy wherever they found it? Either way, many Catholics realised that the Church would have to be reformed if the new religion was not to take over completely.

The Emperor Charles V believed that if the Catholic Church reformed its worst abuses, the Protestants would quickly return to the fold. He wanted the Pope to call a great council, both to reform and make peace with Protestantism. Great councils, made up of cardinals and bishops from all over Europe, had been called before to reconcile splits in the Church.

But the popes were strongly against this. If they carried through these reforms, they would lose a lot of money. Half of the popes' income came from licences and indulgences—the prime targets of the reformers' attacks. Neither did they trust the Emperor, of whose power they were jealous and with whom, in fact, they were often at war. And the popes certainly did not like great councils of the Church which they saw as a threat to their authority. Above all, the papacy did not want to compromise with Protestantism.

So despite the pleas of the Emperor, a Council was not called until 1545, when it met at Trent, on the north Italian border. The meeting of the Council went entirely to the Pope's satisfaction. It spent most of its time defining the doctrine of the Church in a way that rendered any compromise with the Protestants impossible. All the old pillars of medieval Catholicism, such as penances, pilgrimages and the mass, were reaffirmed. So were indulgences. In the words of the Council: 'Since the power of conferring indulgences has been granted to the Church by Christ ... it is to be retained in the Church.' Moreover, the structure of the Church was not changed at all.

Further meetings of the Council in 1562 and 1563 were rather more constructive. By this time Pope Pius IV was dedicated to cleanse the Church of corruption. He was given greater powers to oversee his bishops, while they in turn were given full authority over their clergy. Most importantly, every bishop was instructed to set up colleges in their diocese to train a new generation of priests. The Council also decreed the writing of the catechism—a clear statement for Roman Catholics of what they were expected to believe and do—and a reform of the daily services sung in churches.

One of the inspirations of the Counter-Reformation was Charles Borromeo, Bishop of Milan. He did much to see that the Council's decisions were implemented. He also led a very humble life, working tirelessly for the sick and the poor—a living example that not all in the unreformed Church were rich and corrupt.

The Holy Roman Emperor, Charles V, proposed moderate Catholic reforms to appease the Reformers.

The Inquisition

Although positive things were happening to revitalize Catholicism, much effort also went into rooting out Protestantism. It was believed— by many Protestants as well—that the only way to cleanse a heretic of his terrible sin was to burn him. In 1542, the Roman Inquisition was revived in Italy under a ruthless Inquisitor-General called Caraffa. The Inquisition was given authority to try anyone from any class. Its punishments included imprisonment, confiscation of property and burning at the stake. Under Caraffa's leadership, the Inquisition was used not only to root out Protestant communities in Italy, but also to destroy many Catholics who questioned the Pope's actions or deviated in the slightest from the strict doctrines defined at the Council of Trent.

Pius IV, who was Pope from 1559–65.

An auto-da-fé procession showing victims wearing hats, being carried on poles to be burnt alive.

A similar Inquisition existed in Spain. Originally, it had been set up by the Spanish kings to attack Jews and Muslims. It now turned its attention to Protestants, or anyone else who questioned the Church's authority. After trial, its victims were clad in penitential garments and tall, yellow hats to take part in a ceremony known as the *auto-da-fé* (act of the faith). There was a procession, mass and a sermon and then they were burnt alive—usually in front of huge crowds. The first Spanish Inquisitor called Torquemada, roasted some 2,000 heretics.

The Inquisition also drew up the Index, an official list of forbidden books. Again, it was not only Protestant literature that suffered. Much of the more liberal Humanist works were banned, including the books of Erasmus. In 1555, Caraffa became Pope, and increased the persecution. However, he also did much to clean up his court at Rome, compelling those around him to live simpler lives. He expelled travelling entertainers, forbade dancing and hunting, and restricted luxury. This puritanical streak was continued by his successors, especially Pope Pius V, who was nicknamed 'Friar Wooden Shoe' because of his simple way of life.

47

The Jesuits

In 1521, when the French army was attacking the Spanish town of Pamplone, one of its defenders, called Ignatius Loyola, was critically wounded by a cannonball. During his recovery after the siege, Loyola experienced a religious conversion rather similar to Luther's—though he came to the opposite conclusions. Tormented by guilt over his former involvement in warfare, he determined to reform himself and set out on a pilgrimage to Jerusalem. Returning several years later, he founded a new order called the Society of Jesus.

The Jesuits were typical of the new spirit of Catholicism. Instead of locking themselves away in monasteries, they went out into the community and preached. They converted people and worked with the poor. In this respect they were like other Catholic orders springing up at this time—the Theatines, the Capuchins, the Barbanites, and a new order for women called the Ursulines. But the Jesuits were the most successful.

They became a great missionary society giving direct loyalty to the Pope. Obedience to Catholicism and their order was stressed above all. In the words of Loyola, 'And let each one persuade himself that they that live under obedience ought to allow themselves to be borne and ruled by divine providence working through their superiors exactly as if they were a corpse which suffers itself to be borne and handled in any way whatsoever.' By 1556, they had over 1,500 members who took the Catholic faith to India, China, Japan and the Americas. One of the greatest Jesuits, Father Francis Xavier, travelled in a tattered black robe throughout the Far East—where he is said to have converted over half a million people.

An artist's interpretation of Ignatius Loyola's conversion, depicting Loyola's vision of Christ on the road to Rome.

St Francis Xavier, the great Catholic missionary, 1506–52.

The Jesuits were also at the forefront of efforts to regain territory from the Protestants. They worked with Catholic rulers in Germany, Austria, Bavaria, Hungary and France to re-establish the Catholic Faith. Jesuits set up excellent schools, not only to train priests, but also to educate laymen. Many noble sons throughout Europe attended Jesuit schools, and in this way their influence spread rapidly.

As a result of the efforts of new orders like the Jesuits, the new reforming popes, and loyal Catholic rulers like Charles V and his son Philip II, the Catholic Church not only stopped the spread of Protestantism, but began to regain territory. But Europe was now irreversibly divided, and bloodshed and warfare were to continue between Catholics and Protestants for much of the seventeenth century.

49

7 ENGLAND—A POLITICAL REFORMATION

The Catholic Church in England at the beginning of the sixteenth century was in a similar position to that on the continent, so it is not surprising that new religious ideas took root here also. However, the Reformation that first took place under Henry VIII (1491–1547) was largely political, and the final religious settlement was to be something of a compromise between the extremes of Catholic and Protestant doctrine.

England had a well-established tradition of criticism of the Church. One of the most influential early reformers was a priest called John Wycliffe, a brilliant Oxford scholar in the fourteenth century. He wrote pamphlets criticizing the worldliness of the clergy and produced an English Bible. His followers, nicknamed 'Lollards'—meaning babblers because they preached so much—were persecuted until the sixteenth century, but a few congregations managed to survive particularly in the southern counties.

The Humanist movement was also strong in England. Erasmus spent much of his time there, and his ideas attracted a strong following at the court of Henry VIII. English merchants who had trading links with the Netherlands and Germany were also bringing back more radical ideas. By the 1520s, a group of scholars were meeting regularly at the White Horse Tavern in Cambridge, to discuss Luther's reforms. The tavern soon came to be nicknamed 'Germany'. These men gave their support to a country priest called William Tyndale, who translated and printed the first English Bible at a press in Germany. Copies of his translation were smuggled into England, concealed in bales of cloth.

However, despite efforts by later Protestant writers to try and portray the 1520s as the start of a great popular reformist movement, there is little evidence to support this. There was certainly a general dissatisfaction with the clergy, particularly in London, but nothing to suggest that radical Protestantism had yet made much impact.

The Henrician Reformation
While Luther was confronting the German princes at Worms, King Henry VIII of England was writing a book called *A Defence of the*

Seven Sacraments, directed against the new teachings. For his loyalty, Pope Leo X rewarded Henry with the title of *Fidei Defensor*— 'Defender of the Faith'. Ironically, in view of what happened later, English monarchs still retain this title, which can be seen today on English coins abbreviated to FD.

Henry VIII remained conservative in matters of religion throughout his life. However, he considered himself something of a theologian, so

John Wycliffe (1324–84) who translated the Bible into English.

he encouraged people of differing religious views to attend his court, to take part in debates. Henry's chief minister was Cardinal Thomas Wolsey, who exemplified some of the worst abuses of the Church. He was Bishop of Winchester, York, Durham and Lincoln all at the same time, yet never visited any of these diocese. Nevertheless, although not prepared to reform himself, Wolsey did try to improve the educational standards of the clergy, and suppressed a number of the more scandalous monasteries.

During Henry VIII's reign, the English Church broke away from Rome—but not because of religious differences. Henry had married his dead brother's wife, Catherine of Aragon, in 1509, but unfortunately for her, she was only able to produce a daughter, Princess Mary, to succeed to the throne. Henry desperately wanted a son, for he feared that a female monarch might not have the full support of the nobility. This could lead to a renewal of the bloody civil wars, the Wars of the Roses, which had torn England apart in the previous century.

Consequently, in 1527 Henry asked the Pope to dissolve his marriage. In the normal way, there was no reason why the Pope should not have agreed to this—royal and noble marriages had often been annulled in the past. But at that particular moment, Pope Clement VII had other worries. He was at the mercy of the Emperor Charles V, Catherine's nephew, who had just occupied and sacked Rome. The Pope dared not

William Tyndale presents his English Bible to Henry VIII.

Cardinal Wolsey visiting Leicester Abbey.

offend the Emperor further by insulting his aunt, so he delayed ending Henry's marriage.

But Henry was in a hurry. As the Pope was not proving to be co-operative, the King summoned Parliament, which at his bidding was happy to end the power of the papacy, and appoint Henry 'Supreme Head on Earth of the Church of England'. Henry could now run the Church as he liked. He appointed Thomas Cranmer Archbishop of Canterbury, and by 1533 had divorced Catherine and married Anne Boleyn.

Besides the divorce, Henry's other motive for wanting a break with Rome was greed. The English monasteries were immensely wealthy,

A cartoon of Henry VIII trampling on the authority of the Pope.

and the King was short of money. Thus between 1536 and 1539, Henry's chief minister, Thomas Cromwell, set about dissolving the monasteries and seizing their wealth and property for the Crown. Amongst the nobility and the merchants, and even many of the monks, there was little opposition to Henry's measures. The upper classes willingly bought up the monastic land at cheap prices from the Crown, while the monks received good pensions. Also, there was a strong national feeling in England, and many thought it right that the interference of a foreign pope, hundreds of miles away, should be ended. However, there was opposition in the countryside—particularly in the north, where the monasteries were important as providers of charity and shelter for the poor. A huge popular uprising called the Pilgrimage of Grace began gathering in 1536. Henry only managed to disperse it by promising to reverse his policies—a promise he failed to keep. After the situation had quietened down, its leaders were arrested and executed. Before his death, the Yorkshire leader, Robert Ashe, said of the monasteries: 'The Abbey was one of the beauties of this realm to all men and strangers passing through the same . . .'

Henry had little sympathy with what Protestant reformers were doing on the continent, and having destroyed papal authority and dissolved the monasteries, he did not wish to go much further. An English Bible was introduced in the churches, but an Act of Six Articles passed by Parliament in 1540 was essentially Catholic in doctrine. Nor was the organization of the Church altered. By Henry's death in 1547, England had an independent, national Church, but it was little different from the medieval Church it had replaced.

Monks of a small monastery give up their wealth to Crown officials.

The Edwardian Reformation

Edward VI was only 10 years old when he came to the throne. Rather surprisingly, his father had provided him with a Protestant tutor, Martin Bucer, from Germany, who had a great effect on the young King. Protestant influence was also strong amongst the royal council, appointed by Henry to rule during his son's minority, and under their direction much more radical reforms in the Church were passed.

An Act of Uniformity went through Parliament in 1549 which enforced English services upon the Church. Archbishop Cranmer wrote the Book of Common Prayer in the same year, and it is still used by the Anglican Church today. Most importantly, an attempt was made to bring changes to the local village churches—up until this time these had hardly been altered. A chronicler of the time described some of these changes: 'All images were pulled down through all England, and all the churches were white-limed and the commandments written on the walls. Altars were pulled down and every speaker spoke against all images'. This writer was a Protestant, and was clearly exaggerating. But he does describe accurately what happened in many churches, particularly in the south and east of the country.

Simple villagers must have found these changes in their place of worship most disturbing. Indeed, two rebellions in 1549, one Catholic in outlook and the other Protestant, reflected the divisions in the

The Pilgrimage of Grace, 1536, revealed widespread concern over the dissolution of monasteries by Henry VIII.

St James Church, Morpeth, an example of a highly decorated church.

country at the time. Generally the reforms met with a good deal of resistance, especially in the north, which was still to be predominantly Catholic fifty years later. The old clergy were not sacked from their posts—they were simply told that now they were Protestants. The records of the period show that standards declined, with priests confused about what the new doctrines meant, and ordinary people expressing their disapproval of the change from the old ways by simply giving up going to church altogether. In Gloucester, for example, the local bishop found that of the 311 priests in his diocese, only 79 had a satisfactory knowledge of the new ideas. Of the rest, 168 did not know the Ten Commandments, 133 could not find them in the Bible, and 39 could not even say the Lord's Prayer. As one of Edward's ministers said, 'The old religion is forbidden by law, but the use of the new is not printed in the stomachs of eleven of twelve parts in the realm.'

8 ENGLAND—MARY AND ELIZABETH

As the Protestant bishop, Hugh Latimer and his companion, Nicholas Ridley, were about to be burnt at the stake in Oxford in 1555, Latimer turned to his friend and said, 'Be of good comfort, Master Ridley, play the man, and we shall this day light such a candle by God's grace in England as I trust shall never be put out.'

This quotation gives an essentially Protestant view of the reign of Queen Mary. The persecutions and burnings which were unleashed against the 'martyrs' of the reformed religion have become part of the folk-lore of English history. While there is no doubt that they were very unpopular, they should not be exaggerated, for as we have seen, Protestantism had yet to take firm root in the minds of the English people as a whole.

Latimer and Ridley pray before being burnt at the stake.

Left *Lady Jane Grey, the Nine Day Queen.*

Right *Queen Mary with King Philip II of Spain.*

Catholic revival

Queen Mary succeeded her younger half-brother, Edward VI, in 1553, determined to undo all the recent reforms in the Church of England, and restore the authority of the Pope. A small group of Protestant nobles attempted to put her cousin, Lady Jane Grey, on the throne in place of Mary, but they received little support, and the unfortunate Lady Jane, the Nine-Day Queen, was executed.

The Queen (or 'Bloody Mary') was a rather tragic figure. Much of her youth had been spent in disgrace and unhappiness following Henry VIII's divorce from her mother, Catherine of Aragon. She married and fell in love with King Philip II of Spain, but he was cold and distant towards her, and she produced no child. Moreover, this connection with Spain was very unpopular in England, for it was feared that Spanish authoritarian methods, or even the dreaded Spanish Inquisition, might be introduced in the country.

The defrocked Archbishop of Canterbury, Thomas Cranmer, faced his execution in Oxford, in 1556, as a dignified, loyal Protestant.

In 1554, a solemn mass in Westminster Abbey marked England's return to the Catholic fold. Parliament agreed to re-establish the Pope's authority and to dismantle the Protestant reforms of the previous reign. But it refused to restore the lands of the monasteries. Persecution of Protestants was begun in 1555. Some eight hundred fled abroad to take refuge in centres of Protestantism on the continent, but about three hundred, mostly from London and the east of the country, were burnt to death. One of these was Archbishop Cranmer. In the previous two reigns he had done much to steer England towards Protestantism, and his Book of Common Prayer contains some of the most magnificent prose in the English language. However, on Mary's accession he had recanted, and written a confession denying the new religious ideas. But Cranmer's conscience troubled him greatly, and on the eve of his execution he reaffirmed his Protestant beliefs in a moving sermon, saying 'Forasmuch as my hand offended in writing contrary to my heart, my hand therefore shall be the first punished; for if I come to the fire it shall be the first burnt'. Contemporary woodcuts of Cranmer holding his hand in the flames became famous, and he was acknowledged as a Protestant martyr.

Although the burnings in England were on a far lesser scale than what was happening on the continent, they aroused a profound hatred amongst the people. The Spanish ambassador at the time wrote to warn his master that the 'murmerings' of Londoners against the 'cruel enforcement' of the heresy laws could lead to revolt. It did not in fact, but the persecution left some parts of England with a violent distrust of Catholicism that was to last for centuries.

The Elizabethan Settlement

Mary's childless death in 1559 brought her half-sister, Elizabeth, to the throne. Elizabeth I was by nature moderate and cautious. She wished to bring conciliation to a Church that had undergone the most bewildering series of changes and reversals in the past twenty years. By now there had been three Acts of Uniformity, each telling the people that they had to believe in something different. The clergy had twice been told they were now allowed to marry, and twice this decision had been reversed—which must have caused considerable inconvenience to their poor wives. Everyone was very confused—particularly those living in the countryside.

Queen Elizabeth I, who established the Church of England.

THAT
MANY PRIESTS
AND OTHER CATHOLIQVES
IN ENGLAND HAVE BENE PERSECVTED,

condemned, and executed ; for mere matter of religion : and for
transgreßion onelie of nevv statutes vvhich doe make cases
of Conscience to be treason, vvithout al pretence or sur-
mise of any old treasons or statutes for the same.

CAP. I.

Ow to the principal pointes of
the Libel: we first affirme that
the verie front or title therof,
(importing that no Catholikes
at al, or none of them whom
they haue executed, were persecuted for their religió)is a verie notorious vntruth, and con-
tradictorie to the libellers owne wordes in his dis- *A manifest*
course following where he confesseth vnderhand, *falshood*
vvith con-
that some be corrected othervvise for religion : or (yf they *tradiction*
wil stand in the cótrarie) we appeale to the conscien- *to them-*
ce and knowledge of al the Catholikes and protestan- *selues.*
tes within the Realme, who of their equitie wil ne-
uer denie, that most prisons in England be ful at this
daye, and haue bene for diuers yeares, of honorable
and honest persons not to be touched with anie treason, or other offence in the world, other then their
profession and faith in Christian religion.

Secondlie we say & shal clearlie cóuince, that con-
trarie to the poursute of the same libel, a number haue
bene also tormented, arreigned, condemned and exe-

A

A document opposing the persecution of Catholics under Elizabeth I.

Mary Queen of Scots was executed for plotting with Catholics.

Consequently, Elizabeth's religious settlement was moderate, designed to be accepted by as many people as possible. The Pope's authority was again denied, and Cranmer's Book of Common Prayer re-introduced in the churches. But Elizabeth made it as easy as possible for people to conform, and most did so. She wanted no persecutions, as in her sister's day, for she said she did not wish to 'make windows in men's souls'. If people accepted the most important beliefs of the Church of England, and attended services regularly, they might think, and even worship in private as they liked.

There were, however, two groups who disliked Elizabeth's settlement—the Catholics and the Puritans.

The Catholics

For the Catholics, the religious settlement was obviously unacceptable, because although moderate, it was nonetheless Protestant. Catholicism never died out in England. Even at the end of Elizabeth's reign, nearly half the nobility, and probably the majority of the people still adhered to the old religion.

63

Of God,　　Of Man,　　Of the Divell.

A woodcut of 1640 showing a 'godly' Puritan minister (left) and 'unspiritual' Church of England bishops (centre and right).

However, as Elizabeth's position on the throne grew stronger, and as the threat posed by the Counter-Reformation increased, harsher and harsher measures were enforced against Catholics. These were often prompted by political necessity. In 1570, the Pope excommunicated the Queen, declaring that her subjects should no longer obey her. The heir to the throne, Mary Queen of Scots, was a Catholic, and despite being imprisoned in England, she became the centre of Catholic plots against Elizabeth's life. To combat these dangers, harsh punishments were meted out to Catholic priests and Jesuits who were caught. Between 1577 and 1603, over two hundred were executed, because with the threat of invasion from Spain it was assumed that they were foreign agents. Mary Queen of Scots was herself executed in 1587, the year before the Spanish Armada. But despite their persecution in Elizabethan times and for many years to come, there are still a large number of Catholics in England today.

The Puritans
The other group who were dissatisfied with Elizabeth's settlement were the Puritans. These were really only stricter Protestants, or as one contemporary called them, 'the hotter sort of Protestants'. Ironically, they received much support from some of Elizabeth's own bishops, who also believed the settlement had not gone far enough. Many Puritans had

fled to Geneva during Mary's reign, and wanted to establish Calvinist churches in England. They saw the Church of England as just a step in the right direction.

But Elizabeth, anxious not to provoke a Catholic rebellion or an invasion from outside, did not let them have their way. The churches kept their altars, the priests their robes, and people continued to enjoy themselves on Sundays. Neither was the Queen going to give up her control of the Church—if she accepted a true Calvinist structure, she would be unable to appoint her bishops personally.

The Puritans made their views known increasingly through Parliament. There was a strong group in the House of Commons in the 1580s and 1590s, which continually tried to pass laws to turn England into a more 'godly' society. But they were never a majority, and nor were they prepared to push their views to the outright opposition of the Queen.

This remained true under Elizabeth and her successor, James I. Despite the calls for more reform, no one could deny that England was now a Protestant country. Throughout this period, support was given and alliances made with the Protestants in Holland and Germany. But during the next reign, of Charles I, this policy began to change. Charles initially looked for an alliance with the Spanish, and then with the Catholic French. His bishops also took a much harder line against the Puritans, and religious differences were to play a significant part in the English Civil War (1642–51).

A seventeenth century woodcut, showing the Church of England as the true minister and Puritanism as the false prophet.

The Orthodox true Minifter.   the Seducer and falfe Prophet.

9 THE EFFECTS OF THE REFORMATION

By 1600, Europe was firmly divided into Catholic and Protestant camps. Warfare between the two sides was to continue for much of the next century, and it was only gradually that a spirit of toleration began to grow. One of the most barbaric wars took place in Germany, and was to plunge most of the European states into thirty years of bloody conflict.

It was sparked off in May 1618, when members of the Bohemian Parliament invaded the palace of the Holy Roman Emperor and hurled the royal officials out of the window onto a large dung heap. Although political expediency played its part in the war that followed, it was nevertheless very much a religious conflict between opposing Protestant and Catholic alliances. After thirty years of warfare, which ravaged Germany and rendered most European countries bankrupt, the struggle ended in stalemate with the Peace of Westphalia in 1648.

'Protestant' Catholics and 'Catholic' Protestants
In both the Catholic and Protestant Churches, theological debate about free will and predestination continued, and a wide range of different

Soldiers looting a church of the opposing faith during the Thirty Years War, 1618–48.

The Stuart King, Charles I, 1600–1649.

views flourished. Ironically, some Catholics came to hold views very similar to their Protestant opponents, while some groups in the Reformed Church reached conclusions not dissimilar to mainstream Catholicism. On the Catholic side, a dispute arose in France between the Jesuits, extreme exponents of the idea of free will, and a movement called the Jansenists, who virtually believed in predestination. The Jesuits accused the Jansenists of being Calvinists in disguise.

Amongst the Protestants, a group emerged in Holland called the Arminians. They challenged the idea of predestination, although still claiming to remain in the Protestant camp. The Arminians came to have a great influence in England under Charles I. They were bitterly

Dutch Protestants sailed from Delft in 1620 to join Pilgrim Fathers from other lands, who sought religious freedom in the New World.

attacked by the Puritans for being 'popish', and this division of religious opinion was to contribute towards the outbreak of the English Civil War.

The New World
As we have seen, the impetus of the Counter-Reformation in Catholic countries inspired Jesuit priests to travel all over the world carrying the message of the Faith. At the same time, Protestants from England, Scotland, Germany and Holland were emigrating to North America, taking their new religious ideas with them. Often these emigrants were fleeing from persecution in their own countries, and many were believers in the more extreme versions of Protestantism. The State of Massachusetts, for example, was colonised by English Puritans dissatisfied with the Church of England. The first settlers arrived on the Mayflower in 1620. Every settlement in the colony was led and organized by its Puritan minister, and life centred around the simple churches that they built.

Although fleeing from religious intolerance themselves, these Protestant groups were not always very tolerant of others. When two female members of a different reformed Church, called the Quakers, arrived in Massachusetts, they were beaten as witches. Quakers were perhaps the most Protestant of all the Protestants. They had no clergy and no set services, believing that all should take an equal part as God spoke to the conscience of each one. The Quakers eventually found a haven in Pennsylvania, which Charles II of England granted to William Penn.

The dissenting Protestants who settled in America had a profound influence on the way society in the United States eventually developed. The mid-west of the country today is still known as the 'Bible-Belt', and it is there that the original Protestant ideas still probably survive in their purest form.

The growth of toleration

The Reformation was a period of extreme intolerance. Not only were many Catholics and Protestants killed for their beliefs, but thousands of simple peasants were burnt as witches by both sides. The worst witch-hunts took place in Germany during the Thirty Years War. When an army arrived in an area, hundreds of 'misfits' were rounded up, tortured and burnt. The witch craze is very difficult to explain. One reason may be that the nature of religion changed during the Reformation. The simple superstitions which had been incorporated in the rituals of the medieval Church were now no longer acceptable to either the Protestants or the Counter-Reformation Catholics. Religion had became a sterner business, which aimed more directly at the individual and his relationship with God, than the community's as a whole.

But by the end of the seventeenth century, the idea of toleration was growing. This can partly be explained by necessity. People were

The Thirty Years War caused widespread destruction and slaughter.

tired of wars and persecutions, and it was obvious that neither side could destroy the other. There were some who were beginning to look at the world in a different way. For instance, the work of scientists like Galileo, Descartes and Newton dispelled the idea that the earth was the centre of the universe, and argued that it was not God, but mechanical laws which determined the world. Ironically, this more rational approach was similar in some ways to the Humanists of the early sixteenth century, like Erasmus, whose ideas had been forgotten in the arguments over theology. What emerged from the new way of thinking was the idea of respect for individual conscience—that each individual has the right to choose and follow his or her own religious conviction.

Today, along with other religions, Catholics and Protestants tend to stress their similarities rather than their differences. When Pope John Paul II visited Britain in 1982, he was warmly received by both Protestants and Catholics. He and the Protestant Archbishop of Canterbury joined together for a service in Canterbury Cathedral—a hopeful sign for future unity.

Discoveries by men like Galileo prompted an awakening in scientific and theological thought.

When Pope John Paul II met the Archbishop of Canterbury, Dr Robert Runcie in 1982, there was an obvious warmth between the two leaders.

GLOSSARY

Abdicate   To give up a position of power—usually refers to monarchs.

Absolution   Forgiveness of sins.

Apocalyptical   Referring to the end of the world. The term comes from St John's writing in the Bible in the book of Revelation.

Authoritarian   Strong, often tyrannical rule.

Blasphemy   To speak against God or against the doctrines of the Church.

Christendom   The collective body of Christians throughout the world.

Chronicler   A person who records the events of his period.

Congregation   The collective name of people who regularly attend a particular church.

Convert   To convince someone of the truth of something which they had previously not believed.

Corruption   Dishonest practices such as bribery, or, as in the medieval Church, doing something for financial rather than spiritual ends.

Deride   To dismiss something with scorn.

Diocese   The area administered by a bishop.

Excommunicate   To expel someone from the Church.

Grace   God's favour and forgiveness of sin.

Heretic   Someone who disagrees with the doctrines of the Church. Catholics regarded Protestants as heretics, and vice-versa.

Hierarchy   A system of placing people in ranks or classes graded one above the other.

Layman   Someone who has not been ordained as a priest.

Missionary   A person who travels abroad to convert others to their religion or doctrine.

Orthodoxy   The correct or currently held views on something—particularly Church doctrine.

Pacifist   A person who does not agree with war or fighting.

Penance   A task or punishment given by Catholic priests to sinners before absolving them of their sins.

Persecute   To hunt down and imprison or kill people—usually for religious or political reasons.

Pilgrimage   A journey to a holy place as an act of religious devotion.

Predestination   A belief that an individual's salvation was pre-determined by God at the beginning of time.

Purgatory   According to Catholic belief, a place between heaven and

hell where a soul languishes for a time before achieving salvation.
Purge   To rid an organization of undesirable people.
Recant   To go back on one's previous beliefs or opinions.
Relics   Sacred objects—often the bones of saints.
Sacraments   The seven religious ceremonies of the Catholic church.
Scourging   Being whipped to be cleansed of sin.
Secular   Concerned with matters of the world rather than of religion.
Superstition   Irrational belief about the supernatural or unknown.
Theology   The study of religious ideas and doctrines.

FURTHER READING

Elliot, John Huxstable *Europe Divided* Fontana, 1985
Elton, G. R. *The Reformation—Europe (1517–99)* Fontana, 1969
Green, V. H. H. *Luther and the Reformation* Batsford/New English
    Library, 1964
Harris, Nathaniel *Spotlight on Elizabethan England* Wayland, 1985
Parker, Geoffrey *Europe in Crisis* Fontana, 1979
Phillips, M. M. *Erasmus and the Northern Renaissance* English
    University Press, 1950
Suggett, Martin *Galileo and the Birth of Modern Science* Wayland,
    1981
White-Thomson, S. J. *Elizabeth I and Tudor England* Wayland, 1984

DATE CHART

1483	Birth of Luther at Eisleben	**1546**	Death of Luther
1517	Luther's protest against indulgences	**1547**	Lutheran princes defeated at Battle of Mühlberg
1521	Emperor Charles II summons Luther to the diet of Worms		Death of Henry VIII
		1554	Queen Mary restores the power of the Pope in England
	Henry VIII of England given title of 'Defender of the Faith' by the Pope	**1555**	Peace of Augsberg
1522	Zwingli begins reforms in Zurich		Persecution of Protestants begins in England
1524	Outbreak of Peasants' War in Germany	**1559**	Outbreak of religious wars in France
	Erasmus publishes attack on Luther's theology		Religious settlement of Queen Elizabeth I in England
1529	Diet of Speyer which produced the 'Protest' of the Lutheran princes	**1560**	John Knox establishes Calvinist Church in Scotland
1531	Henry VIII becomes head of the English Church	**1572**	Massacre of St Batholomew in France
1534	Anabaptists take control of Munster		Dutch 'Sea Beggars' capture Brille
1536	Calvin arrives in Geneva	**1587**	Execution of Mary Queen of Scots
	Pilgrimage of Grace takes place in England	**1598**	Edict of Nantes
1538	English Bible issued	**1618**	Outbreak of the Thirty Years War
1540	Ignatius Loyola founds the Jesuits	**1620**	Arrival of the Pilgrim Fathers in Massachusetts
1542	Roman Inquisition revived	**1642**	Outbreak of English Civil War
1545	Opening of the Council of Trent	**1648**	Peace of Westphalia—end of Thirty Years War

INDEX

PICTURE ACKNOWLEDGEMENTS

The illustrations were supplied by: BBC Hulton Picture Library 28; The Courtauld Institute of Art 61; The Mansell Collection 19, 21, 35, 41; Mary Evans Picture Library 4, 5, 10, 11, 13, 15, 16–17, 18, 20, 22, 23, 25, 26, 27, 29, 30, 32, 34, 36, 38, 39, 42, 45, 46, 47, 48, 49, 51, 54, 56, 59 (right), 63, 66, 67, 68, 69; National Gallery 7; National Portrait Gallery 59 (left); Sheridan Photo Library *front cover*; Topham 57, 71.
The remaining pictures are from the Wayland Picture Library.

The author would like to thank his brother, Tom Gibb, for helping to research this book.